MW00595606

SIGHT READING
& RHYTHM
EVERY DAY®

Helen Marlais with Kevin Olson

DAY ONE 1 DAY TWO 2 DAY THREE 3 DAY FOUR 4 DAY FIVE 5

★ LESSON DAY

THE
F·J·H
MUSIC
COMPANY
IN C.
Frank J. Hackinson

Production: Frank and Gail Hackinson
Production Coordinators: Joyce Loke, Philip Groeber, and Isabel Otero Bowen
Cover: Terpstra Design, San Francisco
Text Design and Layout: Terpstra Design and Maritza Cosano Gomez
Engraving: Kevin Olson and Tempo Music Press, Inc.
Printer: Tempo Music Press, Inc.

ISBN-13: 978-1-56939-426-7

ABOUT THE AUTHORS

Helen Marlais' active performance schedule includes concerts in North America, Western and Eastern Europe, the Middle East, and Asia, and her travels abroad have included performing and teaching at the leading conservatories in Lithuania, Estonia, Italy, France, Hungary, Turkey, Russia, and China. She has performed with members of the Pittsburgh, Minnesota, Grand Rapids, Des Moines, Cedar Rapids, and Beijing National Symphony Orchestras to name a few, and is recorded on Stargrass Records®, Gasparo, and Centaur record labels. She has had numerous collaborative performances broadcast regionally, nationally, and internationally on radio, television, and the Internet with her husband, clarinetist Arthur Campbell. She presents workshops at every national convention and is a featured presenter at state conventions. She has been a guest teacher and performer at leading music schools and conservatories throughout North America, Europe, and Asia. Dr. Marlais is the Director of Keyboard Publications for The FJH Music Company Inc. Her articles can be read in *Keyboard Companion, The American Music Teacher,* and *Clavier* magazines.

Dr. Marlais is an associate professor of piano at Grand Valley State University in Grand Rapids, Michigan, where she directs the piano pedagogy program, coordinates the group piano programs, and teaches studio piano. She received her DM in piano performance and pedagogy from Northwestern University and her MM in piano performance from Carnegie Mellon University. She has also held full-time faculty piano positions at the Crane School of Music, S.U.N.Y. at Potsdam, Iowa State University, and Gustavus Adolphus College. Visit: www.helenmarlais.com.

Kevin Olson is an active pianist, composer, and faculty member at Elmhurst College near Chicago, Illinois, where he teaches classical and jazz piano, music theory, and electronic music. He holds a Doctor of Education degree from National-Louis University, and bachelor's and master's degrees in music composition and theory from Brigham Young University. Before teaching at Elmhurst College, he held a visiting professor position at Humboldt State University in California.

A native of Utah, Kevin began composing at the age of five. When he was twelve, his composition *An American Trainride* received the Overall First Prize at the 1983 National PTA Convention in Albuquerque, New Mexico. Since then, he has been a composer-in-residence at the National Conference on Piano Pedagogy and has written music for the American Piano Quartet, Chicago a cappella, the Rich Matteson Jazz Festival, and several piano teachers associations around the country.

Kevin maintains a large piano studio, teaching students of a variety of ages and abilities. Many of the needs of his own piano students have inspired a diverse collection of books and solos published by The FJH Music Company Inc., which he joined as a writer in 1994.

HOW THE SERIES IS ORGANIZED

All rhythmic activities | All sight-reading activities | Place a ✔ when you have been successful!

Each unit of the series is divided into five separate days of enjoyable rhythmic and sight-reading activities. Students complete these short activities "Every Day" at home, by themselves. Every Day the words, "Did It!" are found in a box for the student to check once they have completed both the rhythm and sight-reading activities.

The new concepts are identified in the upper right-hand corner of each unit. Once introduced, these concepts are continually reinforced through subsequent units.

On the lesson day, there are short rhythmic and sight-reading activities that will take only minutes for the teacher and student to do together. An enjoyable sight-reading duet wraps up each unit.

BOOKS 1A AND 1B

Rhythm:

Each unit in book 1A incorporates UNIT counting. UNIT counting (♩ ♩ ♩ ♩ with 1 1 1 2 below) is beneficial because the student learns the exact rhythmic pulse of each particular note. When students have a firm grasp of unit counting, they can easily make the transition to METRIC counting (♩ ♩ ♩ ♩ with 1 2 3 4 below), which is counting the number of beats in a measure.

In book 1A, the student is asked to unit count on "Day One" of each week. The teacher may decide which counting system to use for all other rhythmic activities, although unit counting is recommended for the earliest stages of music making.

Rhythmic activities in books 1A/B include the following:

- Students are asked to count rhythmic examples out loud and clap, tap, point, and march.
- Students learn directional reading.
- Students speak lyrics in rhythm.
- Students add bar lines to excerpts and then count the rhythmic examples out loud.
- Students are asked to pulse with their feet and march in step, to feel a constant pulse.
- Students are asked to clap rhythmic examples by memory, an excellent ear training and memory exercise.
- Students tap different rhythms in both hands.
- Students learn and drill $\frac{2}{4}$, $\frac{3}{4}$, and $\frac{4}{4}$ time signatures.

Fingering:

Alternate fingering is provided so that students learn to play patterns starting on other fingers instead of always resorting to the thumb. This helps to promote a good hand position with a strong hand arch.

Reading:

Students start the series by recognizing the following guide notes: treble G, bass F, and middle C (both clefs). After that, they read patterns starting a second above or below these guide notes. Students then progress into sight reading patterns starting on guide notes an octave above and below middle C. This is followed by patterns starting a third above or below all of the guide notes, then a fourth above or below all of the guide notes they have learned up to this point.

The keys of C, G, F, D, and A major are learned in books 1A and 1B, as well as the intervals of harmonic and melodic seconds, thirds, fourths, and fifths.

Sight Reading activities include the following:

- The student learns to "plan" for note and rhythmic accuracy, correct articulations, and a good sound.
- Helpful suggestions guide students to think before they play, and not stop once they have started!
- Students are asked to sing the melody before actually playing some of the excerpts, which encourages them to maintain a constant pulse and the forward motion of the musical line.
- Students circle and analyze intervals, patterns, and key signatures before playing.
- The metronome is incorporated once a week.

Developing these important skills lays the proper foundation for music making and fosters stellar piano playing. A student who sight reads well has the skills to progress rapidly and enjoy success. *Sight Reading & Rhythm Every Day*® is a sure way to produce the positive results that motivate students.

FJH148

TABLE OF CONTENTS

Unit 1

DAY ONE

New Concepts: 4/4 time signature; starting on guide note C; ♩ ♩; melodic 2nds

 Rhythm—Clap the following rhythmic examples and count out loud!

Place a ✔ when you have been successful!

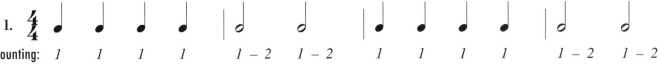

Unit Counting: 1   1   1   1   1 – 2   1 – 2   1   1   1   1   1 – 2   1 – 2

2.   1 – 2   1   1   1 – 2   1   1   1   1   1   1   1 – 2   1   1

 Sight reading—Tap and count the rhythm before playing. Then play the melody without stopping, even if you make a tiny mistake. Play with a big, warm sound!

DAY TWO

 Rhythm—Draw arrows (up or down) to show the direction of the musical line, and circle each group of repeated notes. Point to each note as you count along.

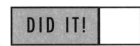

 Sight reading—Play the following without stopping, observing all pitches and rhythms.

FJH148

3
DAY THREE

Rhythm—Speak the lyrics in rhythm while you point to each note.

DID IT!

1. Hur - ry up! It's time for school! We don't want to miss the bus!

2. Look - ing out my win - dow, I can see a rain - bow.

Sight reading—Tap the rhythm before playing. Play and sing or hum the melody, and don't stop!

1. 2 (1)

2. 2 (1)

4
DAY FOUR

Rhythm—Add bar lines to the following rhythms.
When you have finished, clap and count each line twice.

DID IT!

1.

2.

Sight reading—Clap and count each melody line before playing.
Can you memorize the examples and clap the rhythm without looking?

1. 2 (1)

2. 2 (1)

Rhythm—Tap the upstem notes with your right hand and the downstem notes with your left hand for the following rhythmic examples. Count loudly with energy in your voice!

DID IT!

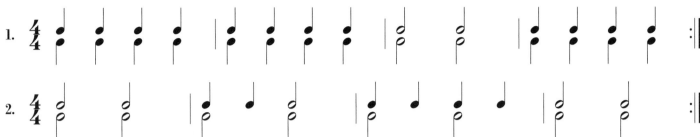

 Sight reading—With the metronome set at ♩ = 92, clap or tap the following examples. Then play these using the same metronome speed. Always look ahead!

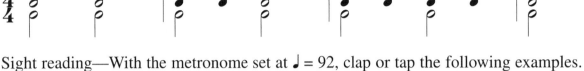

 ★ LESSON DAY

 Rhythm—Point to the example you hear your teacher clap. Listen carefully! Then clap and count both examples.

 Sight reading—Your teacher will play one of the following melodies. Point to the melody that you hear. Then choose an example to sight read for your teacher.

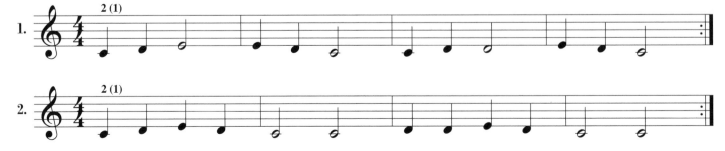

FJH1489

Ensemble Piece

DID IT!

Before you begin this duet, clap and count the rhythm of the student part. In order for the soldiers to march, the rhythm must be steady. Keep your eyes on the music and count as you play.

Soldiers Marching

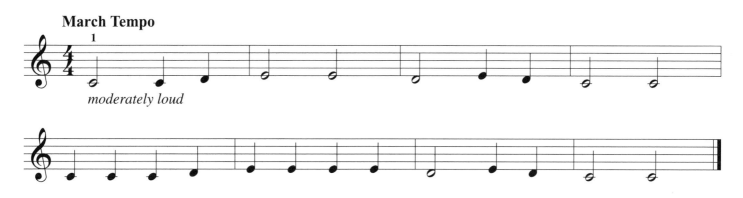

Teacher accompaniment (student plays one octave higher than written)

? After playing, ask yourself, "Did I play with a steady beat?"

Unit 2

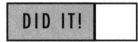

DAY ONE

 Rhythm—Clap the following rhythmic examples and count with energy! | DID IT! | |

Sight reading—Tap and count the rhythm before playing. Then play the melody without stopping, even if you make a tiny mistake. Play with a big, warm sound!

1.
2.

DAY TWO

 Rhythm—Draw arrows (up or down) to show the direction of the musical line, and circle each group of repeated notes. Point to each note as you count along. | DID IT! | |

1. $\frac{3}{4}$

2. $\frac{3}{4}$

Sight reading—Be sure to relax your wrist while playing. Feel the steadiness of the beat as you play.

1.
2.

3
DAY THREE

Rhythm—Speak the lyrics in rhythm while you point to each note.   DID IT!

1. $\frac{4}{4}$

Pi - rates   bold   in   the   night,   Come   on   board   and   see   the   sight!

2. $\frac{3}{4}$

Mu - sic   can   make   the   world   a   much   bet - ter   place.

Sight reading—Tap the rhythm before playing.
Counting *while you play* will help you keep a steady beat.

1.

2.

4
DAY FOUR

Rhythm—Add bar lines to the following rhythms.   DID IT!
When you have finished, clap and count each line twice.

1. $\frac{3}{4}$

2. $\frac{3}{4}$

Sight reading—Silently play these melodies on the top of the keys.
Play slowly enough so that you do not stop.

1.

2.

Rhythm—Tap the following rhythmic examples.
Count out loud with confidence.

DID IT!

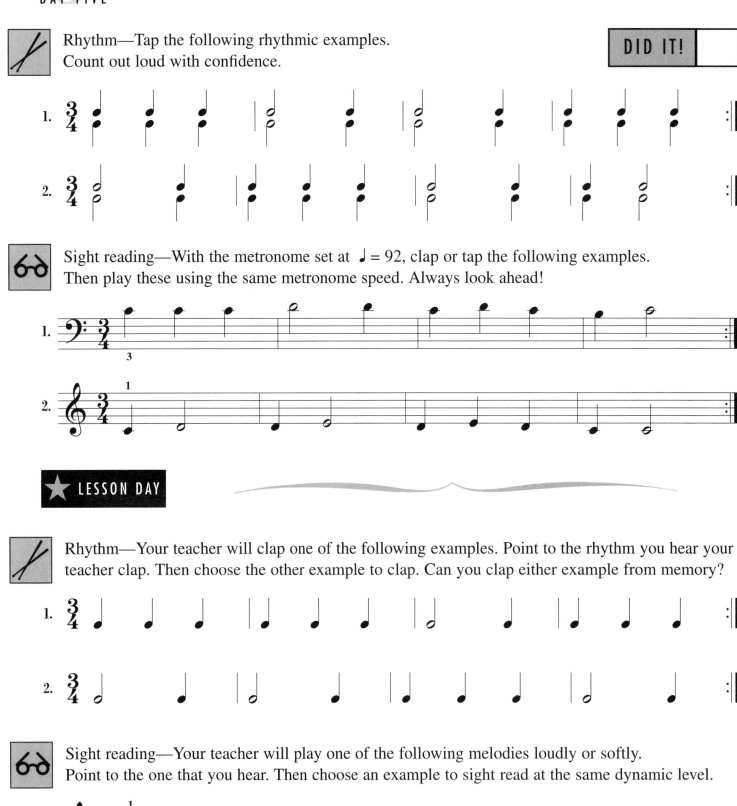

Sight reading—With the metronome set at ♩ = 92, clap or tap the following examples.
Then play these using the same metronome speed. Always look ahead!

⭐ **LESSON DAY**

Rhythm—Your teacher will clap one of the following examples. Point to the rhythm you hear your teacher clap. Then choose the other example to clap. Can you clap either example from memory?

Sight reading—Your teacher will play one of the following melodies loudly or softly.
Point to the one that you hear. Then choose an example to sight read at the same dynamic level.

FJH148

Ensemble Piece

DID IT!

Before you begin this duet, tap and count the rhythm of the student part. Decide if the notes step up or down, or repeat. Keep your eyes on the music and count as you play! Reading the title of this duet, will your part be slow or fast? Loud or soft?

Lazy River Song

Teacher accompaniment (student plays one octave higher than written)

? After playing, ask yourself, "Did this piece sound lazy?"

Unit 3

DAY ONE

 Rhythm—Clap the following rhythmic examples and count with confidence!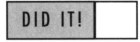

Sight reading—Circle the guide notes before you begin. Then tap and count the rhythm before
playing. Lastly, play the melody without stopping, even if you make a tiny mistake.
Play with a big, warm sound!

DAY TWO

 Rhythm—Draw arrows (up or down) to show the direction of the musical line,
and circle each group of repeated notes. Point to each note as you count along.

Sight reading—After you have circled the guide notes, clap and count the melodies.
Then play with a big, warm sound!

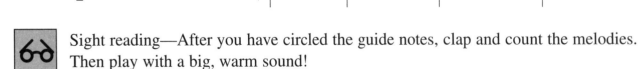

14

FJH1489

Rhythm—Speak the lyrics in rhythm while you point to each note.

DID IT!

1.
Rain - drops fall - ing on the ground. Pit - ter, pat - ter is the sound.

2.
Pea - nuts, pop - corn, sold at the ball - game.

Sight reading—Tap the rhythm before playing. Play the melody without stopping, observing all pitches and rhythms. Play with a big, warm sound!

1.

2.

Rhythm—Add bar lines to the following rhythms.
Then stand and march in place to the rhythms you see. Accent every downbeat.

DID IT!

1.

2.

Sight reading—How are these two examples similar?
Clap and count each melody line before playing.

1.

2.

Rhythm—Tap the following rhythmic examples.
Count loudly with energy in your voice!

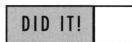
1.

2.

 Sight reading—Silently play these melodies on top of the keys at ♩ = 76.
Then play them with a big sound, keeping a steady beat, listening to the rise and fall of the melody.

 LESSON DAY

 Rhythm—Clap one of the following rhythmic examples for your teacher.
Ask your teacher to decide which rhythm you clapped.

1.

2.

 Sight reading—Circle all of the G guide notes in both examples below.
Then play these melodies for your teacher. Play one example loud, the other, soft.

FJH1489

Ensemble Piece

Before you begin this duet, point to the notes and count the rhythm of the student part.
Then, keeping your eyes on the music, count as you play.

Irish Ballad

With warmth

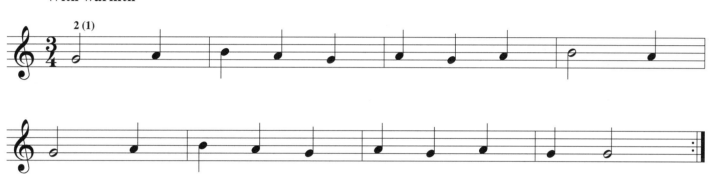

Teacher accompaniment (student plays one octave higher than written)

? A *Ballad* is a story. After playing, ask yourself,
"What kind of story is this?"

FJH1489

17

Unit 4

New Concepts: 𝅗𝅥.; *f* and *p* dynamics

DAY ONE

 Rhythm—Clap the following rhythmic examples and whisper the counting! 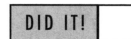 DID IT!

1.

2.

 Sight reading—Point to the notes and count these examples before playing. Circle the G ($\oint$) and F ($\mathcal{9}$) guide notes. Then play the melody without stopping, keeping your eyes on the music.

1.

2.

DAY TWO

 Rhythm—Draw arrows (up or down) to show the direction of the musical line, and circle each group of repeated notes. Point to each note as you count along.  DID IT!

1.

2.

 Sight reading—Count the rhythm of these melodies silently while following the music with your eyes. Plan the sound before playing!

1.

2.

18

FJH1489

3
DAY THREE

Rhythm—Speak the lyrics in rhythm while you point to each note.

DID IT!

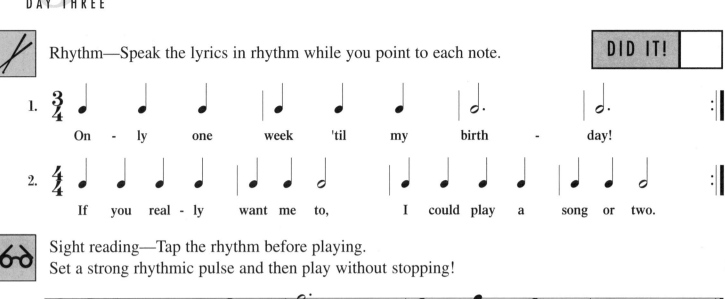

1.
On - ly one week 'til my birth - day!

2.
If you real - ly want me to, I could play a song or two.

Sight reading—Tap the rhythm before playing.
Set a strong rhythmic pulse and then play without stopping!

4
DAY FOUR

Rhythm—Add bar lines to the following rhythms.
Then tap the rhythm on your legs, accenting every downbeat.

DID IT!

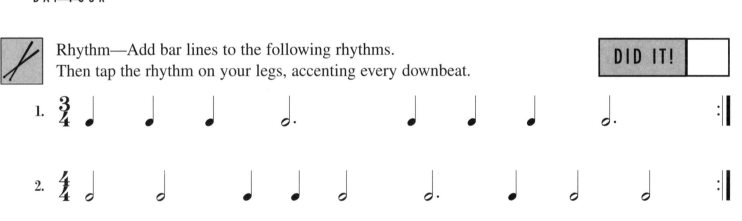

Sight reading—Play the first pitch. Can you sing or hum the melody in your head?
Plan the sound before you play.

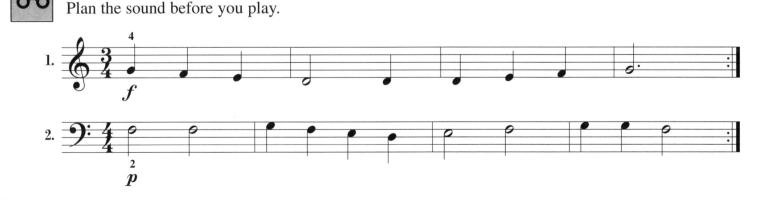

Rhythm—Tap the following rhythmic examples.
Count out loud with confidence!

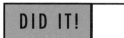

1.

2.

 Sight reading—Silently play these melodies on top of the keys at ♩ = 76. Keep a steady beat while you play and listen to the rise and fall of the melody. Plan the sound before beginning.

1.

2.

 LESSON DAY

 Rhythm—Add notes to make sure each measure is complete. Then tap and count out loud.

1.

2.

 Sight reading—Circle all of the dotted half notes (♩.) in both examples below.
How are these two examples similar? How are they different? Play them both with a steady pulse.

1.

2.

FJH1489

Ensemble Piece

DID IT!

Before you begin this duet, clap and count the rhythm of the piece. Decide if the notes step up or down, or repeat. Would you expect the sounds from a trombone to be *piano* or *forte*? Keep your eyes on the music and count as you play.

The Trombone Lesson

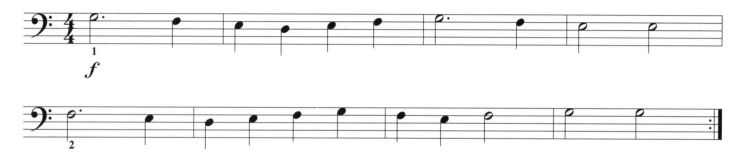

Teacher accompaniment (student plays as written)

? After playing, ask yourself, "Did the trombonist play with a smooth sound and a steady beat?"

Unit 5

New Concepts: melodic thirds;
legato phrasing

DAY ONE

Rhythm—Clap the following rhythmic examples and count with energy!

Sight reading—Point to the notes and count these examples before playing.
Circle all of the melodic thirds. Then play the melodies, keeping your eyes on the music.
Play the notes within the slurs *legato*, or smoothly.

DAY TWO

Rhythm—Draw arrows (up or down) to show the direction of the musical line,
and circle each group of repeated notes. Point to each note as you count along.

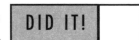

Sight reading—Clap and count the rhythm before playing. Circle all of the melodic thirds.
Then play without stopping, with a big, warm sound.

FJH1489

3

DAY THREE

Rhythm—Speak the lyrics in rhythm while you point to each note.

DID IT!

1. I am like a drum-mer, hear me keep a stea-dy beat for you.

2. I hear the ice cream man com-ing down the street to-day!

Sight reading—Tap the rhythm before playing. Plan the melodic thirds.
Then play the melody without stopping!

4

DAY FOUR

Rhythm—Add bar lines to the following rhythms.
Then stand up and tap the rhythms with your feet!

DID IT!

Sight reading—Circle all of the melodic thirds below. Silently and steadily play the melody on top of the keys. When you think you can play these examples without stopping, go ahead and play out loud!

DAY FIVE

Rhythm—Tap the following rhythmic examples.
Count loudly with energy in your voice!

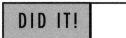
DID IT! ☐

1.

2.

Sight reading—With the metronome set at ♩ = 92, clap or tap the following examples. Then play these examples at the same metronome speed. Then repeat the process with the metronome set at ♩ = 104.

1.

2.

★ LESSON DAY

Rhythm—Clap the upstem notes at the same time your teacher claps the downstem notes.
Then switch parts!

1.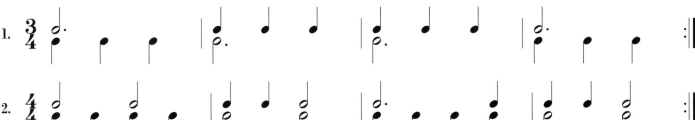

2.

Sight reading—Circle all of the melodic thirds in the examples below. Block (playing the thirds *together*) with the correct fingering. Listen for a *legato* sound within the slurs.

1.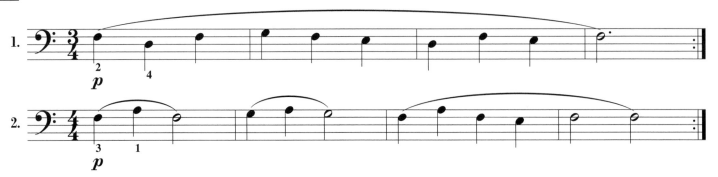

2.

FJH1489

Ensemble Piece

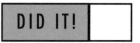

Before you begin this duet: 1) Tap and count the rhythm of the student part. 2) Block the melodic thirds (play them together). 3) Plan the sound. 4) Keep your eyes on the music as you play.

The Tattle-Tale

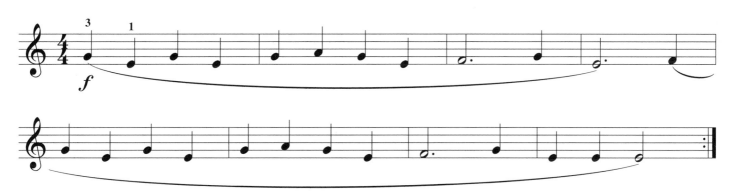

Teacher accompaniment (student plays one octave higher than written)

 After playing, ask yourself, "Did I play this piece with a steady beat?"

FJH1489

Unit 6

New Concepts: use of the fifth finger;
key signature for C and G major

 Rhythm—Clap the following rhythmic examples and count with confidence! DID IT!

 1.

1   1   1   1   1 – 2 – 3   1   1 – 2 – 3   1   1   1   1 – 2

2.

 Sight reading—Point to the notes and count these examples before playing.
Both melodies are in G major so be sure to place your fingers in G position before starting.
Are there any melodic thirds in the two examples?

1.

f 5

2.

p

 Rhythm—Draw arrows (up or down) to show the direction of the musical line, and circle each group of repeated notes. Point to each note as you count along. DID IT!

1.

2.

 Sight reading—Clap and count the rhythm before playing. Then play with energy!

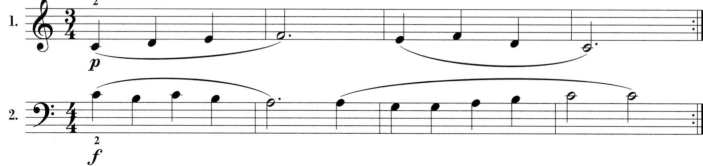

1.

p

2.

2

f

DAY THREE

Rhythm—Speak the lyrics in rhythm while you point to each note.

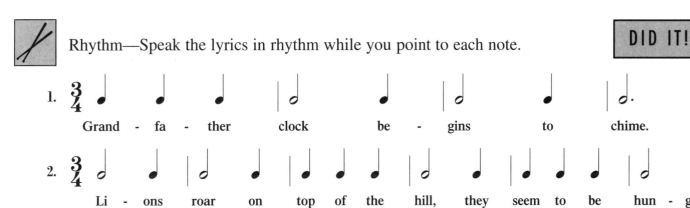

1. Grand - fa - ther clock be - gins to chime.

2. Li - ons roar on top of the hill, they seem to be hun - gry!

Sight reading—Tap the rhythm before playing. Circle all of the G's before you begin.
Are there any F sharps? If so, plan these before playing.

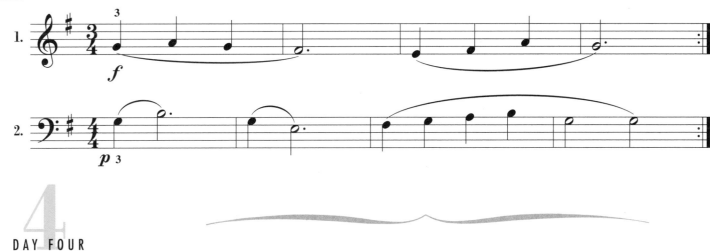

DAY FOUR

Rhythm—Add bar lines to the following rhythms.
Then stand up and march to the rhythms! Accent every downbeat.

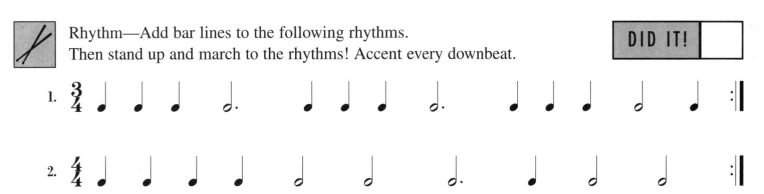

Sight reading—Clap and count each melody line before playing.
Can you clap the rhythm of each example *without* looking at the music?

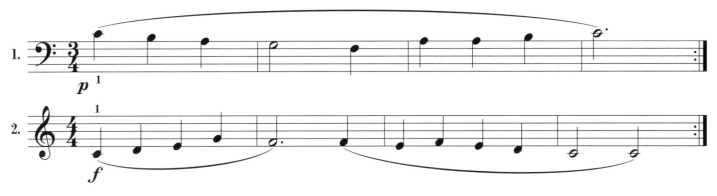

FJH1489

DAY FIVE

 Rhythm—Tap the following rhythmic examples.
Count out loud with confidence!

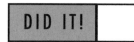

DID IT!

1.

2.

 Sight reading—With the metronome set at ♩ = 92, clap or tap the following examples. Then play these examples at the same metronome speed. Then repeat the process with the metronome set at ♩ = 104.

 LESSON DAY

 Rhythm—Clap these rhythms with your teacher clapping the same rhythm one measure behind you. This will create a round. Remember the repeats, and keep a steady beat!

 Sight reading—Your teacher will play one of the following melodies. Point to the melody that you hear. Then choose the other example to sight read for your teacher, remembering to plan the sound before you begin.

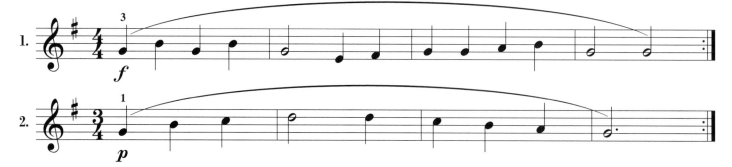

28

FJH1489

Ensemble Piece

DID IT!

Before you begin this duet, point to the notes and count the rhythm of the student part.
Circle all of the melodic thirds. Keep your eyes on the music and keep it steady as you play.

Canyon Shadows

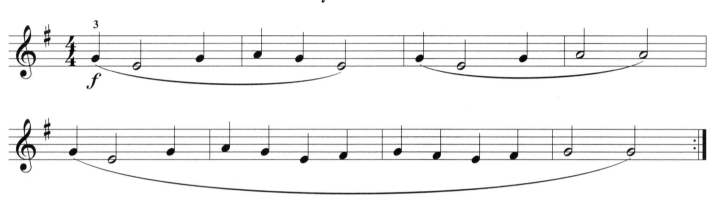

Teacher accompaniment (student plays one octave higher than written)

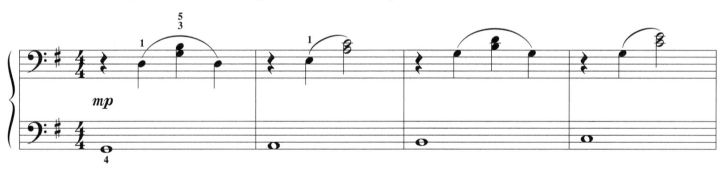

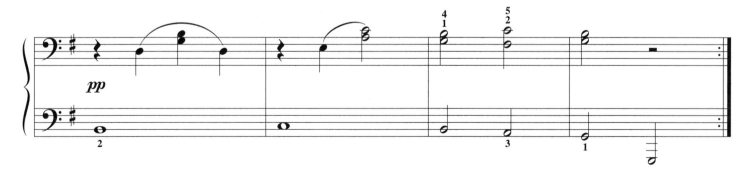

? After playing, ask yourself, "Did I play this duet with a big, warm sound?"

Unit 7

New Concept: key signature for F major

DAY ONE

Rhythm—Clap the following rhythmic examples and count out loud!

DID IT!

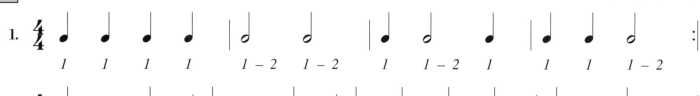

Sight reading—Point to the notes and count these examples before playing.
Both melodies are in F major so be sure to place your fingers in F position.
Are there any B flats? Play the melodies without stopping!

DAY TWO

Rhythm—Draw arrows (up or down) to show the direction of the musical line, and circle each group of repeated notes. Point to each note as you count along.

DID IT!

Sight reading—Be sure to relax your wrist while playing.
Plan the sound and the tempo before you begin.

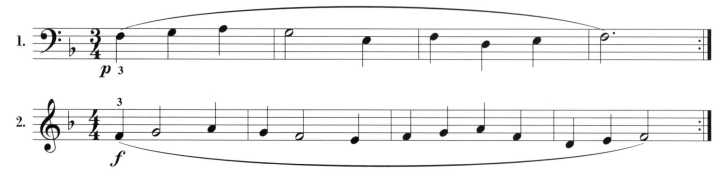

30

FJH1489

DAY THREE

Rhythm—Speak the lyrics in rhythm while you point to each note.

DID IT!

1. How ma - ny stars are up in the sky?

2. I am eat - ing pea - nut but - ter sand - wich - es for lunch to - day!

Sight reading—Tap the rhythm before playing. Decide if the melody goes up or down by steps (seconds) or by skips (thirds). Then play the melody with a strong rhythmic pulse.

DAY FOUR

Rhythm—Add bar lines to the following rhythms.
When you have finished, clap and count each line twice.

DID IT!

Sight reading—Silently play these melodies on the top of the keys.
Play slowly enough so that you do not stop. Always look ahead.

Rhythm—Tap the following rhythmic examples.
Count loudly with energy in your voice!

 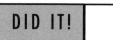

 Sight reading—With the metronome set at ♩ = 112, clap or tap the following examples.
Then play these examples at the same metronome speed. If you make a mistake, keep going!

★ LESSON DAY

 Rhythm—Make up a melody in F position to play for your teacher using the rhythms below.

 Sight reading—Your teacher will play one of the following melodies.
Point to the melody that you hear. Then choose an example to sight read for your teacher.

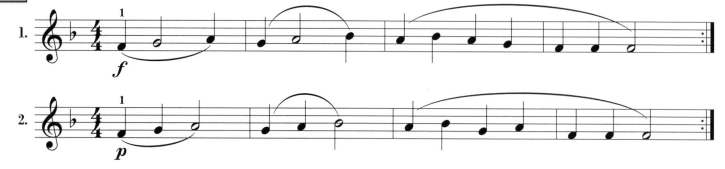

Ensemble Piece

DID IT!

Before you begin this duet, point to the notes and count the rhythm of the student part.
Decide if the melody line goes up by seconds or thirds. Keep your eyes on the music and not on
your hands as you play.

Northern Lights

Teacher accompaniment (student plays one octave higher than written)

with pedal

? After playing, ask yourself, "Did my sound glow?"

Unit 8

New Concept: whole note (○)

1 DAY ONE

Rhythm—Clap the following rhythmic examples and count with energy!　**DID IT!**

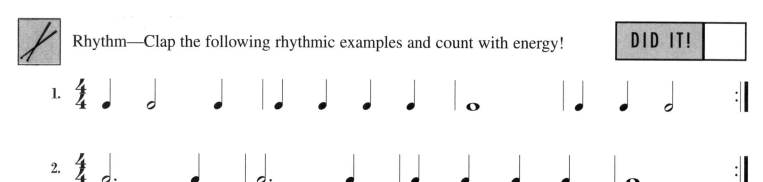

Sight reading—These melodies are in G and F major. Block (play together) all of the melodic thirds, and then all of the melodic seconds. Then plan your tempo and begin!

2 DAY TWO

Rhythm—Draw arrows (up or down) to show the direction of the musical line, and circle each group of repeated notes. Point to each note as you count along.　**DID IT!**

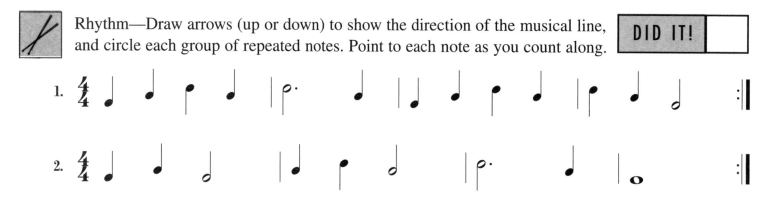

Sight reading—Clap and count the melodies. Then play with a big, warm sound!

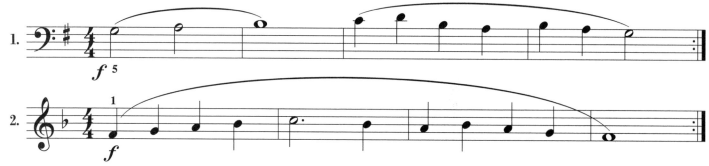

34

FJH1489

3
DAY THREE

Rhythm—Speak the lyrics in rhythm while you point to each note.

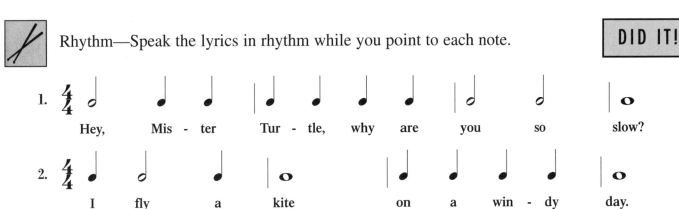

DID IT!

1. 4/4
Hey, Mis - ter Tur - tle, why are you so slow?

2. 4/4
I fly a kite on a win - dy day.

Sight reading—Tap the rhythm before playing.
Set a strong rhythmic pulse and then play without stopping!

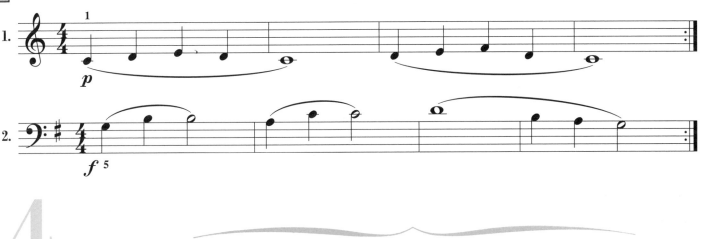

4
DAY FOUR

Rhythm—Add bar lines to the following rhythms.
Then tap the rhythms on your legs, accenting every downbeat.

DID IT!

1. 4/4

2. 4/4

Sight reading—Plan ahead! Study the rhythms and keys of the following examples.

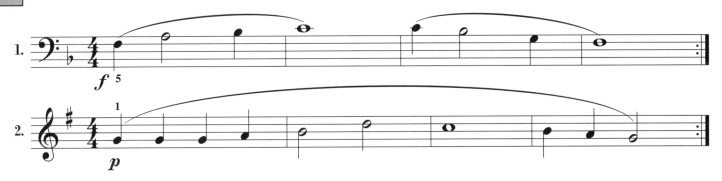

DAY FIVE

Rhythm—Tap the following rhythmic examples.
Count out loud with confidence!

DID IT!

Sight reading—With the metronome set at ♩ = 112, clap or tap the following examples.
Then play these examples at the same metronome speed. If you make a mistake, keep going!

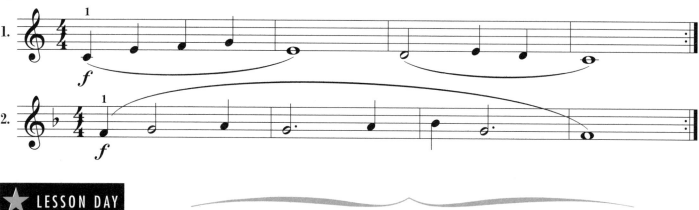

★ LESSON DAY

Rhythm—Point to the example that you hear your teacher clap.
Listen carefully, then count and clap each example for your teacher.

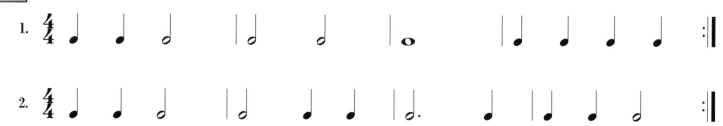

Sight reading—Plan ahead! Notice the key signatures and the rhythms. Decide if the melody line
goes up or down by seconds or thirds (steps or skips). Play with a steady pulse!

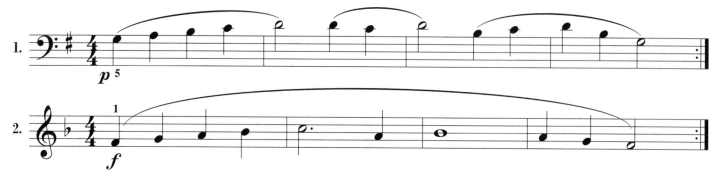

FJH1489

Ensemble Piece

DID IT!

Before you begin this duet, notice the key, the time signature, and the steps (2nds) and skips (3rds) in the melody line. Decide the tempo to fit the title of the piece. Look at the music and not at your hands while playing.

Snoring Sloths

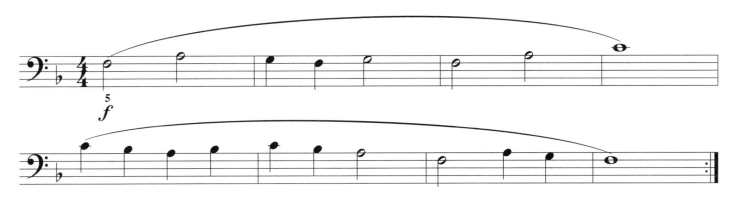

Teacher accompaniment (student plays one octave lower than written)

? After playing, ask yourself, "Did this piece have a big snoring sound?"

Unit 9

DAY ONE

Rhythm—Clap the following rhythmic examples and whisper the counting! DID IT!

Sight reading—Tap and count the rhythm before playing.
Block (play together) the melodic thirds before playing the examples as written.

DAY TWO

Rhythm—Draw arrows (up or down) to show the direction of the musical line, and circle each group of repeated notes. Point to each note as you count along. DID IT!

Sight reading—Count the rhythms of these melodies silently while following the music with your eyes. Then play without stopping!

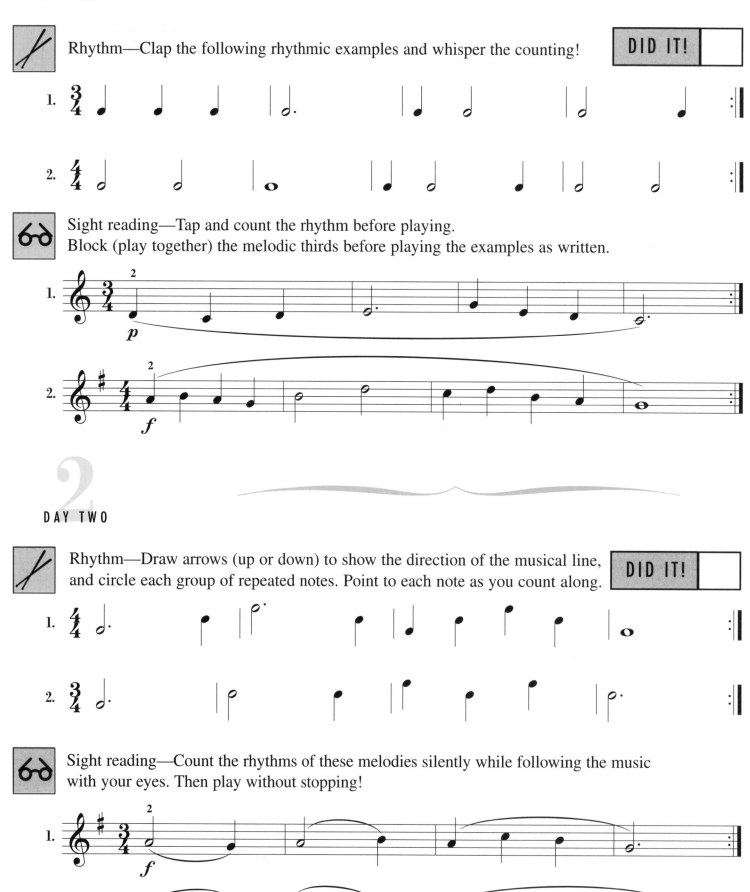

38

3

Rhythm—Speak the lyrics in rhythm while you point to each note.

DID IT!

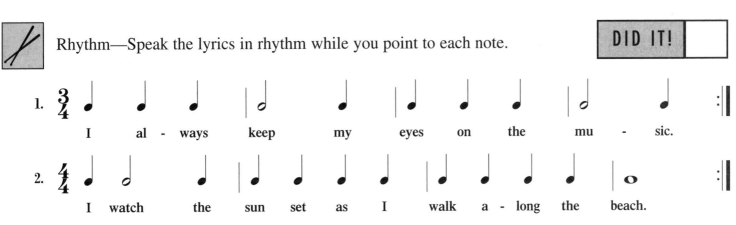

1. I al - ways keep my eyes on the mu - sic.

2. I watch the sun set as I walk a - long the beach.

Sight reading—Tap the rhythm before playing. Play the melody without stopping, observing all pitches and rhythms. Plan the sound before playing.

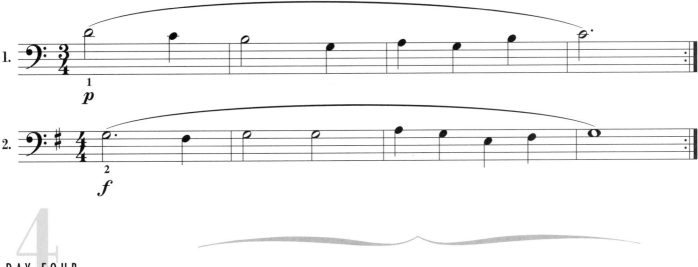

4

DAY FOUR

Rhythm—Add bar lines to the following rhythms.
When you have finished, clap and count each line twice as fast.

DID IT!

Sight reading—Play the first pitch of Example 1. Tap or clap the rhythm while you sing the melody in your head. Then play and sing the melody. Do the same with Example 2.

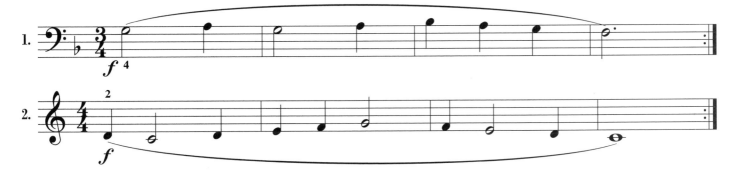

DAY FIVE

Rhythm—Tap the following rhythmic examples.
Count loudly with energy in your voice!

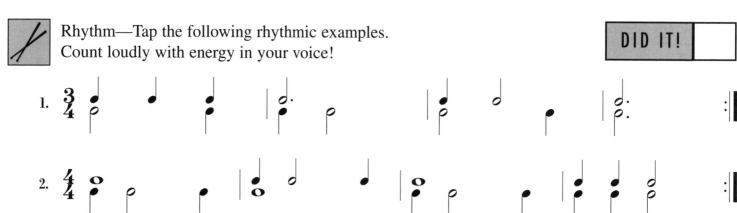

Sight reading—Silently play the melodies on the top of the keys at ♩ = 116.
Keep a steady beat while you play and listen to the rise and fall of the melody.

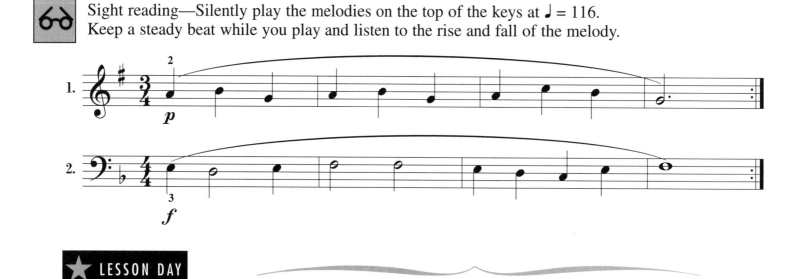

★ LESSON DAY

Rhythm—Your teacher will clap one of the following examples. Point to the rhythm you hear your
teacher clap. Then choose an example to clap. Can you clap either example from memory?

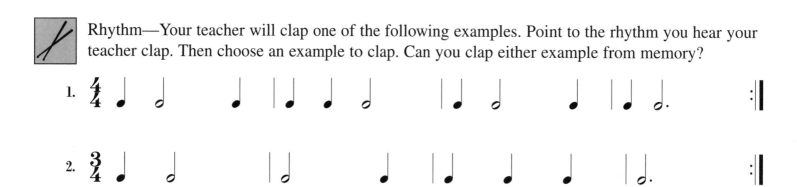

Sight reading—Circle the bass clef F guide note and the treble clef G guide note in the examples
below. Then play the examples.

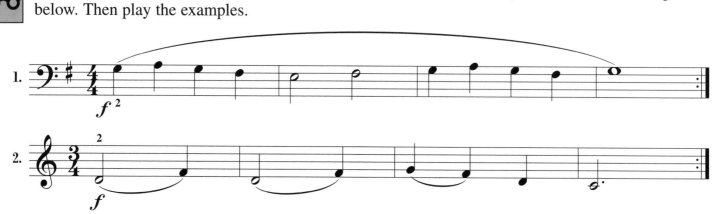

FJH148

 **LESSON DAY**

Ensemble Piece

DID IT!

Before you begin this duet, clap and count the rhythm of the student part. Is the first note a second above or below guide note G? Would you expect a piece with the title *Right-Hand Rag* to be bright and cheerful or slow and sad?

Right-Hand Rag

Teacher accompaniment (student plays one octave higher than written)

? After playing, ask yourself, "Did I keep my eyes on the music the whole way through?"

JH1489

41

Unit 10

DAY ONE

New Concepts: *mp* and *mf* dynamics
General review

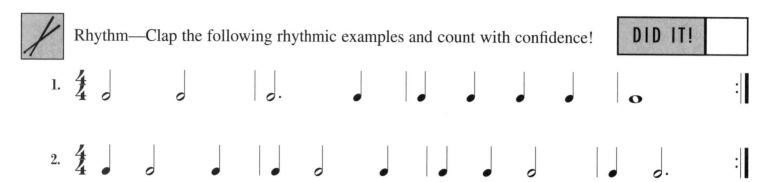

Rhythm—Clap the following rhythmic examples and count with confidence!   **DID IT!**

Sight reading—Tap the rhythm before playing. Circle the guide notes of G (𝄞) and F (𝄢).
Then play the melodies without stopping.

DAY TWO

Rhythm—Draw arrows (up or down) to show the direction of the musical line,
and circle each group of repeated notes. Point to each note as you count along.   **DID IT!**

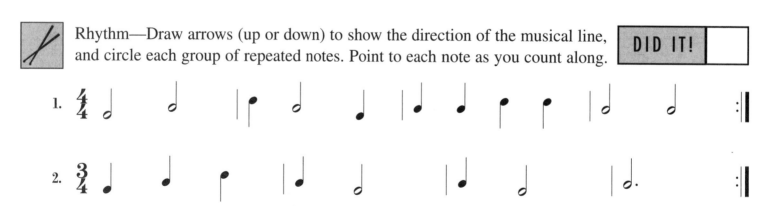

Sight reading—Clap and count the rhythm before playing.
Plan the sound and play with a steady pulse!

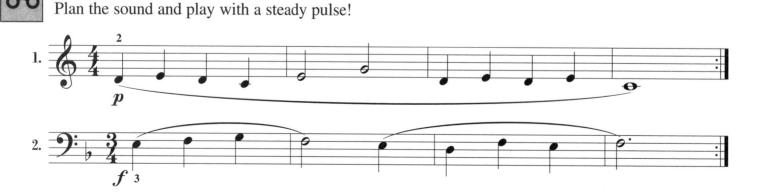

3

Rhythm—Speak the lyrics in rhythm while you point to each note.

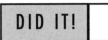

1. $\frac{3}{4}$

Six   times   six   is   thir - ty   six.

2. $\frac{4}{4}$

Hum - ming birds love nec - tar   from our gar - den flow - ers.

Sight reading—Tap the rhythm before playing. Circle all of the guide notes.
Decide how you want each example to sound before you begin.

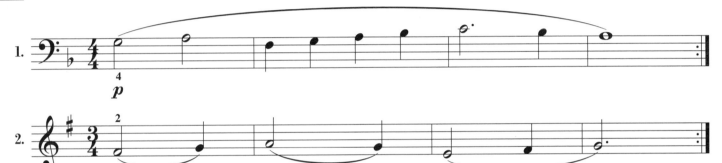

4

Rhythm—Add bar lines to the following rhythms.
Then stand up and stomp the rhythms with your feet.

1. $\frac{4}{4}$

2. $\frac{4}{4}$

Sight reading—Plan ahead. Study the rhythm and direction of the melody line.
Then play the following examples with energy!

DAY FIVE

Rhythm—Tap the following rhythmic examples.
Count out loud with confidence!

 Sight reading—Silently play the melodies on the top of the keys at ♩ = 116.
Keep a steady beat while you play and listen to the rise and fall of the melody.

Rhythm—Clap the following examples. For all of the "X" notes, snap your fingers
or knock on the wood of the piano for a new sound!

 Sight reading—Circle all of the ♩. and o notes in both examples below.
Then play both melodies and listen for a *legato* sound within the slurs.

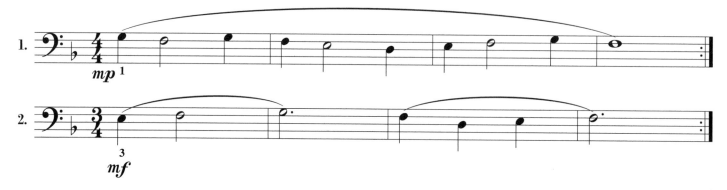

44

FJH1489

Ensemble Piece

Before you begin this duet, silently play the student part on the fallboard. Plan ahead:
notice things like the key signature, dynamics, fingering, and the B flat in the second line.

Riverwalk

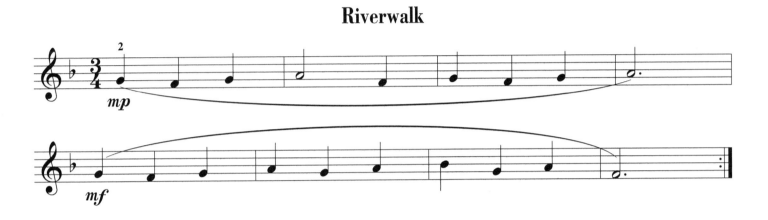

Teacher accompaniment (student plays one octave higher than written)

? After playing, ask yourself, "Did I play this with a *legato* sound?
Did I keep going no matter what?"

Sight Reading and Rhythm Review

Rhythm—Clap and count the following eight-measure examples out loud. Keep a steady pulse, and don't stop!

DID IT! ☐

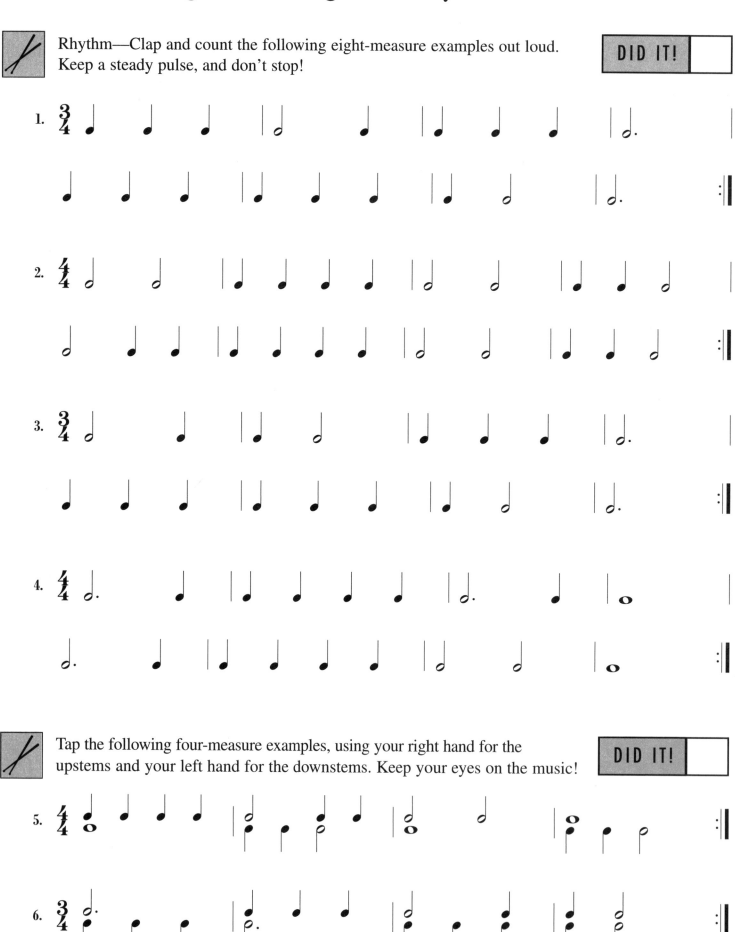

Tap the following four-measure examples, using your right hand for the upstems and your left hand for the downstems. Keep your eyes on the music!

DID IT! ☐

FJH148

• Play the following guide notes, then write the guide note names underneath each note.

DID IT!

• Play the following melodic intervals, then write in the intervals you played.

Example:

2nd up

DID IT!

• Fill in the names of the following key signatures.

no sharps or flats   1 sharp   1 flat

DID IT!

• Play the following pentascales, hands together, ascending and descending.

DID IT!

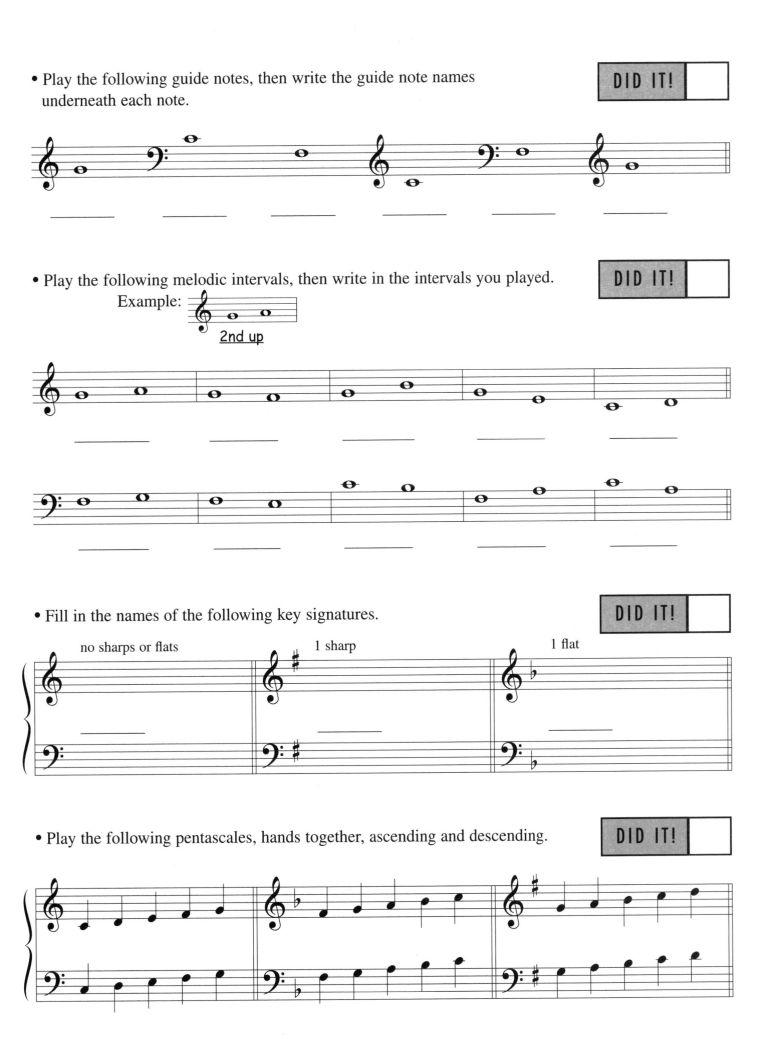

Additional Sight Reading Exercises

Unit 1: Notice the repeated notes before playing.

Unit 2: Silently count before playing.

FJH14

8.

9.

10.

Unit 3: Find the guide notes before playing.

11.

12.

13.

14.

15.

Unit 4: Play silently first.

16.

17.

18.

19.

fingering? ___

fingering? ___

20.

Unit 5: Find the melodic 3rds before playing.

21.

FJH148

fingering? ___

fingering? ___

Unit 6: Notice the 2nds and 3rds before playing.

fingering? ___

29.

30.

31.

32.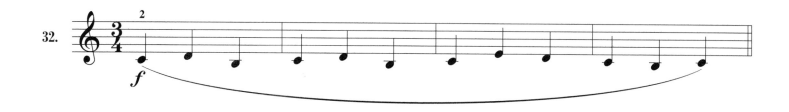

Unit 7: Count out loud while playing.

33.

34.

35.

FJH1489

36.

37.

38.

Unit 8: Notice the 2nds and 3rds before playing.

39.

40.

41.

42.

Unit 9: Circle the Middle C, Treble G, and Bass F guide notes before playing.

50.

Unit 10: Count aloud while playing. Always look ahead!

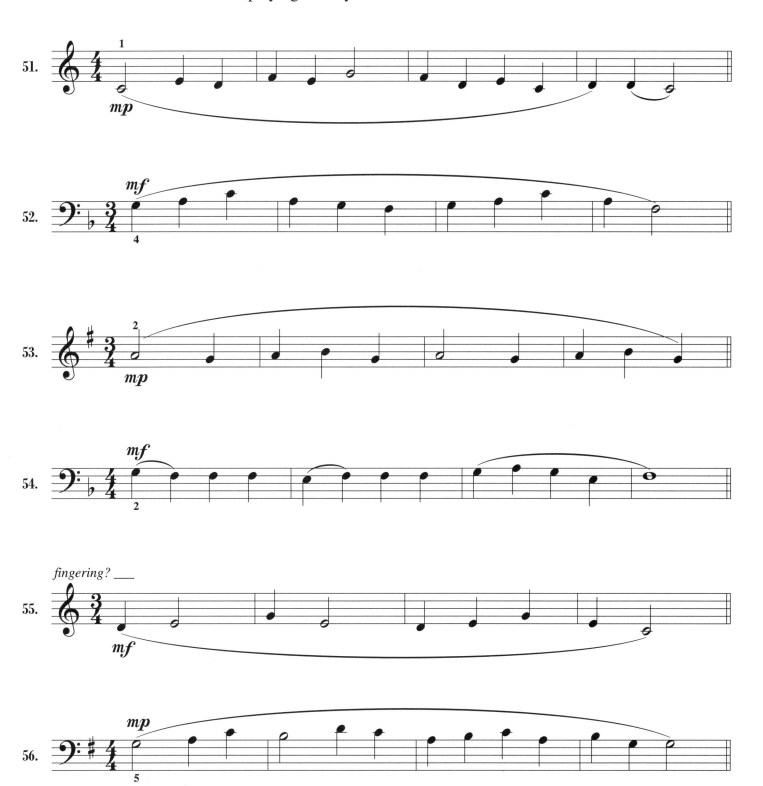

51.

52.

53.

54.

fingering? ___

55.

56.

Certificate of Achievement

_____

has successfully completed

SIGHT READING & RHYTHM EVERY DAY®

BOOK 1A

of The FJH Pianist's Curriculum®

You are now ready for **Book 1B**

_____
Date

_____
Teacher's Signature